MW01089980

# Contents

*We grieve because we loved.*
*Love endures all things.*

# Coping with Holiday Grief

*Can I Make the Holiday Season Disappear?*

Dora Carpenter and Christina Ferguson

Copyright © 2014
All Rights Reserved

Wishing you a holiday season of cherished
memories and hope for a fulfilled life of peace,
comfort, and joy. We thank you for
allowing us to be a part of your life as you
travel your grief journey.


Love and Gratitude,
Dora and Christina

*Cherish the Memories and Embrace the Future*

# Introduction

How do you cope with the happy holiday season when you are heartbroken from the death of a loved one? While you are drowning in tears of sadness, it seems that everyone else has forgotten about your loss. The sights, sounds, and smells of the season confront you wherever you go. The rituals of family togetherness, gift giving, decorations, and celebrations really touch the heart of the void that has been left. The reality hits that the holidays you once treasured with your loved one will never be the same.

This unscheduled event of loss has placed itself on your calendar and you can't reschedule or delete it. This is not the way you think your holiday season ought to be, yet you are being forced to acknowledge and accept it.

A question frequently asked by coaching clients is, "Can I make the holiday season disappear?" No, you can't; however, *Coping with Holiday Grief* shares helpful tools and tips for getting through this time of year and finding hope for a meaningful future.

Make this holiday season a time of reflection and renewed hope. Smile as you ponder the many lessons learned, memorable times shared, the laughter and tears, advice received, the hugs and kisses, and the legacy left.

It is our sincere desire that you will find peace and comfort as you allow yourself to feel the presence of your loved one this holiday season, and we extend love and gratitude to you as you embrace meaning and purpose in your new life going forward.

# Anticipation of the Holiday Season

During the holiday season, while others are celebrating gift giving, family togetherness, traditions of thanksgiving, and holiday joy, you may be challenged with feelings of sadness, loneliness, and emptiness. This time of the year is known as the season to be jolly, but you are facing the reality that your life as it was has been changed forever.

The anticipation of the holidays without your loved one is often harder than the actual holidays. The first few years are usually the most difficult, but even many years later, the pain and sadness surface during this time of year.

Since we are all unique individuals, your holiday grief will be unique to you. Remember, no one can tell you how to grieve because no one knows the exact relationship you shared with your loved one. Although you might receive many suggestions and offers of advice, this is the time for you to remember and reflect as you choose to.

Statistics show that it can take, on average, five to eight years to recover from the loss of a loved one. With a commitment to receiving support and taking action steps to move forward, it doesn't have to take that long.

Following are some tips that will help you:

- Set a personal affirmation, or intention, for this holiday season (see Suggested Holiday Affirmations).

- Be kind, gentle, and patient with yourself.

- Don't overwhelm yourself with responsibilities. Decide what you feel will be important to do.

- It is okay to say "no" to holiday invitations.

- Accept that the holidays will not be the same, so don't try to make things as they were. This will only lead to compounded grief and disappointment.

- Don't shy away from complete holiday traditions. Allow yourself to do what you can do. If you can't decorate the whole house, decorate a room, a corner, a shelf, etc.

- Search for ways to blend the past with the present, i.e., include some of your loved one's favorite holiday ornaments with your new ones.

- Give yourself and your family permission to enjoy the holidays and have fun. This should not be considered disrespectful to the deceased.

- Do something special for someone else.  Adopt a needy family for the holidays.

- Be sure to take care of yourself. Grief can cause tremendous stress on your body.  Eat well, exercise, and get rest.

- Talk with a trusted friend, spiritual advisor, therapist, counselor, or a grief coach. Choose someone who is non-judgmental, will listen, and will offer you hope, encouragement, and support.

# Can I Handle It?

What does one really mean when asking, "Can I make the holiday season disappear?" or "Can I skip this time of year?" or "Can I go to sleep and wake up in January?" That feeling of not wanting to be present usually simply equates to the thought or feeling that "I just can't handle the memories of what used to be a celebration of family togetherness, joy, fun, shopping, laughter, memories… and is no longer."

You might even experience envy, although not intended, as you see others enjoying the festivities of the season. You might experience anger at others, yourself, the deceased, God, or anyone who is associated with the death.

Please understand that the grief journey and grief work is a process. You cannot read this book, or do the suggested activities, and expect the painful emotions of loss to magically disappear. You can, however, find your way through this wilderness by acknowledging your emotions, accepting the loss, and taking action steps to move forward.

Being aware of some of the pitfalls that can keep you stuck will help you during this time. Here are five of the common pitfalls of holiday grief:

• Anxiety and Stress: The pain and absence you might feel is natural and normal; however, focusing only on these feelings creates more anxiety. The mind, body, and spirit all work together, so the broken heart, if not addressed, can wreak havoc on your whole body. Let the pain and hurt out so you can make room for hope, love, and gratitude.

• Holiday Traditions: When your family circle has been broken, you might have low energy or little desire to participate in holiday events. Some might even get an award for pretending to be okay. Don't participate in activities that will cause you anxiety and stress. If attending events, don't be afraid to speak of your loved one. Others may shy away from doing so because they don't want to upset you, so when you do, it frees them to speak, honor, and celebrate with you.

- Guilt and Regret: These are two of the more difficult emotions to overcome. Getting beyond the "should have's, if only's, ought have's, why didn't I's" takes time, patience, and work. Whether these thoughts are rational or not, the feelings are very real and must be acknowledged and released. Beating up and blaming yourself for something you did or didn't do, or blaming someone else for something they did or didn't do, can cause you great mental and physical harm. You must take action to move beyond these potentially devastating emotions.

- Fear of the Future: Fear and faith can't live in the same house, so choose one. Loss of a loved one can create fear due to new responsibilities, loss of income, security, emotional support, companionship, faith, self-esteem, and sense of belonging... just to name a few. Everyone has it and as long as you continue to grow, you will experience fear. However, if not dealt with, it can paralyze you. You must do the grief work to transfer fear, and uncertainty into confidence in your ability to handle the future.

- Moving Forward: As with all situations in life, you have choices. If you have a flat tire, you can choose to have it changed and move forward, or do nothing and stay stuck on the side of the road. The pain of loss and the process of moving forward can be overwhelming and a very difficult path to walk. You don't have to walk it alone. Reach out for help.

# The 5-Step Recipe for Coping with Holiday G.R.I.E.F.

**G**ive yourself permission to grieve.

**R**emember to honor the life and legacy of your loved one.

**I**ncorporate new traditions into old traditions.

**E**mbrace meaning and gratitude in your new life going forward.

**F**ear, Forgiveness, and Faith.

# Step 1

## Give yourself permission to grieve.

An integral part of the grief process is acknowledging our feelings of loss, so give yourself permission to grieve. Choose to make this holiday season a special time to remember your loved one. As you do so, focus on your loved one's life and not the death. Listen to your heart as you find joy in the tears. Smile and remember the good times shared.

*Notes*_____

_____

_____

_____

_____

_____

_____

_____

_____

# *Step* 2

## Remember to honor the life and legacy of your loved one.

Of course we remember the lives of our loved ones, but how can we honor them? In what way can you make someone else's life better in honor of your loved one? What legacy did your loved one leave that you can share? What lessons have you learned as a result of your loved one's death that you can incorporate into your own life?

*Notes*_____

_____

_____

_____

_____

_____

_____

_____

_____

_____

# Step 3

## Incorporate new traditions into old traditions.

You can keep some holiday traditions alive in ways to comfort you as you accept your new reality. Begin to incorporate new traditions into the holiday season. You might purchase a new ornament and place it on the holiday tree next to a favorite ornament of your loved one.

*Notes*_____

_____

_____

_____

_____

_____

_____

_____

_____

_____

_____

# *Step 4*

**Embrace meaning and gratitude in
your new life going forward.**

You have been extended membership in a
club that you never asked to join, and
your life will never be the same again;
however, your life can be meaningful.
You have an obligation to live your life
for the rest of your life.  What are you
grateful for today?  What legacy will you
leave your loved ones?

*Notes*_____

_____

_____

_____

_____

_____

_____

_____

_____

_____

# *Step 5*

## Fear, Forgiveness, and Faith.

What are you afraid of? Yes, you know that life continues and that you must move on; but, what about fear of the future without your dear loved one? Fear and uncertainty of your future can bring on increased emotions of anxiety and stress.

The Serenity Prayer reads: God grant me the serenity to accept the things I cannot change; courage to change the things I can; and wisdom to know the difference.

What about forgiveness? Forgiveness frees you from emotional suffering. Letting go of hurts or perceived wrong doings opens you to allow and receive the abundance of life that is available to you. Unforgiveness can paralyze you and have adverse effects on your emotional and physical wellbeing. This holiday season forgive everyone, including yourself, for everything associated with the loss.

What role does faith play in the grief process? Although one might question their faith during this time, grief can oftentimes deepen one's faith when relying on it for peace, hope, and strength. Begin each day with prayer, meditation, or whatever ritual works to connect you with your Source. Be open to allow and receive the abundance of love that is available to you. You might also focus on the true meaning of this time of year. Your belief system can be the catalyst that gives you the courage to move forward and seize new possibilities.

*Notes*_____

_____

_____

_____

_____

_____

_____

# What About the Children?

Death is a confusing topic for children and it is challenging to comprehend the idea that someone is never coming back, especially during special days such as birthdays and the holidays. There are many questions that follow a death, and one must be able to provide support to children as they begin to accept the reality of this loss in their lives.

It is important to recognize and be aware that children grieve also. Their grief may appear to look different from adult grief, but it is a necessary process for healing and moving forward with their lives. If not addressed and supported through the grief experience, a child's unresolved grief might manifest in other, sometimes unhealthy, ways later in life. A common misconception is to hide your emotions from children to keep up the façade that everything is okay, or that you are strong. Talking and sharing your feelings with children shows that you are human and that it is okay to express your feelings about the loss of a family member.

Death often becomes the elephant in the room in order to protect children. One of the most important things you can do during this holiday season and beyond is to listen to your child and talk about their feelings.

Patience and honesty is also a key factor when dealing with children who have experienced a loss. Death is not easy to talk about, especially when grieving yourself. Be patient, as young children may not understand right away and will often ask many questions as they try to comprehend this deviation from the norm in their lives. Be as honest as possible, but also consider the age of the child, when discussing the death. Be careful, however, not to fabricate stories although it might seem the right thing to do at the time. Remember, children grow up to be adults and will recall not only the loss, but the stories they were told about the death.

Include children in as many age-appropriate conversations as you strive to make this a journey that the family will travel together. Feel free to talk about their loved one and let them share their emotions and feelings as they like. It may sometimes be uncomfortable, but it is normal and a necessary process. There might be times when the child may not want to talk about the person or the death. As difficult as this may be, respect their space and continue to give words of encouragement and support as you allow them to work through it.

During the holidays, include special activities for the children to remember their loved one. Blend old traditions with new ones that the children help create. Remind them of the legacy left and why it is important to celebrate life and build their own legacy.

One of the most important things that you can do this holiday season for a child who has lost a loved one is to be there for them. Listen without trying to fix their grief. Sit with them even if they don't want to talk. Show them that you are there for them, that you love them, and that you support them. Following the death of a loved one, a child's sense of security might be shaken. Reassure them that you are there for them. Be sure that they understand they are not alone.

Reaching out for support is not only for adults, but an effective means to help children cope with grief. Because their grief can be hidden, it is beneficial to have them participate in a children's grief support program to ensure that they are able to express their feelings.

# What Lies Ahead?

Although your brightest light may be dimmed right now, you must first believe that you will see bright light again – maybe not the same light, but a new light, a different light, maybe even a brighter light. Confess to yourself that you will not become a victim to this inevitable process of life, but that you will be victorious as you pursue your own path. Begin by saying YES to life! Make a decision to replace any heartbreak with gratitude. As you do, you will shift more quickly towards enjoying your new life.

My mantra for life is, "Everything in life is temporary, including life itself; so, decide to say YES! to the gift of now." Now... the present... the gift... that is all that you have. Yesterday is gone and tomorrow is the future (which is not guaranteed to you); however, you do have right now.

What will you do?  What will you say and to whom?  Who will you love?  What gift, talent, or treasure will you share?  Who will you help?  How will you serve?  What legacy will you leave your family, your friends, your community, the world?

I charge you with using this holiday season to adopt a renewed mindset as you begin to build purpose, meaning, love, and gratitude going forward.  You are special, you are a gift, and your life counts.  You have a responsibility to share it.  Let your light shine bright so that others might see and be blessed by it.

What lies ahead for you?  Use this time to honor your loved one by creating a fulfilled life during this holiday season, the new year, and beyond!

# Suggested Holiday Affirmations

An affirmation is a strong positive statement declared to be true.  Even if you don't believe it or feel it at the time, I encourage you to do it anyway.  The subconscious mind is powerful and only responds to what you feed it.  Feed it negative, you get negative.  Feed it positive, you get positive.  This practice just might change your life.

Begin and end each day during this time by repeating your holiday affirmation.  You can use all or parts of the following affirmation or create your own.

"I embrace each day of the holiday season with love and gratitude.  Love for myself, which I will extend to others.  Gratitude for the many blessings I receive daily.

I accept that this holiday will be different, but will have new meaning.

I let go of thoughts of how I wish things were this holiday.

I will make this holiday season a time of peace and reflection.

I will cherish the gift that my loved one's life and legacy has been to me.

I am powerfully, fearlessly, and wonderfully made and capable and deserving of a fulfilled, happy, and meaningful life.

I seek to find what I am to learn, where I am to grow, and how I am to serve.

I look forward to my future with new expectations.

I maintain good self-care with proper nutrition, exercise, relaxation, sleep, and stress management.

I devote time for spiritual meditation and reflection.

I embrace love, peace, and joy in myself, my family, my friends, and the world.

I am happy that I am making a difference in my life and the lives of others.

I now breathe new life into my heart and soul and commit to greet each day with love and gratitude."

# Suggested Holiday Activities

- Visit a place that you visited with your loved one during the holiday season. Go alone or with someone who supports what you are doing.

- Visit the cemetery and place a wreath or holiday tribute on the gravesite.

- Set a place setting at the table in honor of your loved one.

- Do something that your loved one always wanted to do but never did, or an activity that your loved one enjoyed, i.e., golfing, parasailing, shopping, etc.

- Take a trip to a destination you've never visited.

- Get together with family and/or friends for a gathering or celebration for the "good ole days." View photo albums, videos, and memorabilia.

- Volunteer at a nursing home, children's center, hospital, soup kitchen, etc. There are organizations that coordinate these holiday visitation programs.

- Buy a gift in honor of your loved one and donate it to a charitable organization.

- Dedicate a special ornament or light a memorial candle to celebrate the light of love that forever lives in your heart.

- Pamper yourself, i.e., spend the day at the spa or attend a weekend retreat.

- Write a holiday goodbye or thank you letter to your loved one expressing your feelings.

- Take a day to reflect on your own life. Focus on your positive gifts, aspirations, talents, and abilities.

- Reflect on your spiritual beliefs. Attend a holiday service or religious celebration.

- Go to see a play, movie, or holiday event.

- Reach out to another person who is grieving this holiday season.

- Perform a random act of kindness, i.e., buy someone a cup of coffee, pay the toll for the person in the car behind you.

- Send a thank you card or a letter of gratitude to someone who has made a positive impact in your life.

- Start a brand new holiday tradition for yourself or your family.  Get creative with ideas.

- Put together a holiday memories scrapbook.  You might make this a family project.

- Have a cry party.  Set aside a special hour or so, go to a quiet place with a box of tissues, light a candle, play soft music or a favorite song….. and cry. Shed your tears of heartache and tears of joy.

- Take a drive to "nowhere." Start driving with no set destination in mind. Enjoy everything along the way.

- Take time to meditate and reflect. Offer a prayer of gratitude for having loved and been loved.

- Create a "gifts of gratitude" arts and crafts project which depicts all the gifts your loved one shared with you, i.e., fun, happiness, humor, affection, love, companionship, etc.

- Research options for going back to school, taking up a new career, starting a business.

- Journal your progress or write a book.

- Have a private party. Sing out loud and dance around the house.

- Start a new hobby that is creative and fun such as drawing, painting, dancing, knitting, photography, etc.

- Join a social networking group or support group.

- Dine alone at a restaurant. Choose a favorite restaurant of your loved one or one that you've never visited.

- Send thank you notes to the people in your life who stood by you when you needed them.

# About Dora Carpenter

Dedicated to inspiring and empowering individuals for personal and professional success, Dora Carpenter is known for challenging and motivating clients to take action and move forward in life transitions, grief, and fear. Her gentle and empathetic approach is articulated in her coaching, writing, speaking, and mentoring.

Working in the death care industry and assisting hundreds of families with making final arrangements for loved ones birthed her passion for coaching. Dora says "too many hopes and dreams are buried in the cemetery" and her personal mantra is "Everything in life is temporary, including life itself. Decide to say Yes! to the gift of now."

Dora Carpenter is a certified life coach, certified grief coach, certified consumer's funeral consultant, and founder of The ANIYA Group Life Coaching Center. She is also a licensed Feel the Fear and Do It Anyway® trainer. Dora Carpenter has been recognized by the National Association of Distinguished Professionals as a professional in her field and has been a guest on podcasts, radio, and television. Learn more about Dora Carpenter at www.doracarpenter.com.

# About Christina Ferguson

Christina says, "Life does not come with an instruction manual and is simply a day-to-day experience." One usually has a mental picture of how their life is supposed to look, but it doesn't always go as planned. What happens then?

During the course of marriage; a miscarriage; separation; the gift of reconciliation; a second miscarriage; then, to being separated again and ultimately divorced, Christina found herself in a space of chaos and confusion. "This is life as it is NOW, but what are you going to do about it?" is Christina's personal mantra of empowerment. She will challenge you to look at your curve balls of life, own your truth, and create your personal story.

Christina Ferguson is a graduate of Hampton University and received her coach training from the World Coach Institute. She is co-founder of The ANIYA Group Life Coaching Center, certified to teach "Yes You Can" self-esteem workshops for women of all ages, and is a Feel the Fear and Do it Anyway® licensed trainer. Learn more about Christina Ferguson at www.speakoutwithchristina.com.

The ANIYA Group Life Coaching Center
Washington, D.C.
www.theaniyagroup.com

*Find more information on grief programs and*
*resources at The Grief Corner at*
*www.doracarpenter.com*

Made in the USA
Coppell, TX
04 September 2021

61730895R00026